Dark River

A play with music for young people

Alexa Romanes

A SAMUEL FRENCH ACTING EDITION

FOUNDED 1830

SAMUELFRENCH.COM
SAMUELFRENCH-LONDON.CO.UK

FOR PRODUCTION ENQUIRIES

UNITED STATES AND CANADA
Info@SamuelFrench.com
1-866-598-8449

UNITED KINGDOM AND EUROPE
Plays@SamuelFrench-London.co.uk
020-7255-4302/01

Each title is subject to availability from Samuel French, depending upon country of performance. Please be aware that *DARK RIVER* may not be licensed by Samuel French in your territory. Professional and amateur producers should contact the nearest Samuel French office or licensing partner to verify availability.

MUSIC USE NOTE

Licensees are solely responsible for obtaining formal written permission from copyright owners to use copyrighted music in the performance of this play and are strongly cautioned to do so. If no such permission is obtained by the licensee, then the licensee must use only original music that the licensee owns and controls. Licensees are solely responsible and liable for all music clearances and shall indemnify the copyright owners of the play(s) and their licensing agent, Samuel French, against any costs, expenses, losses and liabilities arising from the use of music by licensees. Please contact the appropriate music licensing authority in your territory for the rights to any incidental music.

IMPORTANT BILLING AND CREDIT REQUIREMENTS

If you have obtained performance rights to this title, please refer to your licensing agreement for important billing and credit requirements.

DARK RIVER

First performed by Broughton Junior Drama Group on 16th May, 1999, with the following cast of characters:

King	William Lloyd
Plug	Mark Banas
Jericho	Emma Bebb
Whippet	Thomas Hoskins
Mouse	Michelle DuBlack
Annie	Hannah Powell
Frank	William Bebb
Sal	Isobel Gammer
Maggie	Virginia Fowler
Jack	Katy Waller
Goose	Christopher Paul
Muvver	Emma Bebb
Coster 1	Joanne Tidy
Coster 2	Beth James
Coster 3	Virginia Fowler
Bootlace Seller	Mark Banas
Gingerbread Seller	Katy Waller
Soup Seller	William Lloyd
Peg	Joanna Tidy
Sir Henry	Thomas Hoskins
Liza	Beth James
Mrs Saunders	Liz Ottley
Jack-in-the-Green	Mark Banas
Fiddle Player	Jonathan Lloyd

Costers, Chimney Sweeps, Passers-by
Serena Barnes, James Gulliver, Jonathan Lloyd, Matthew Paul, Briony Peach, Luke Waller

Directed by Alexa Romanes
Designed by Clare Shearman

CHARACTERS

King, a pickpocket
Plug ⎫
Jericho* ⎬ King's gang
Whippet ⎭
Mouse ⎫
Annie ⎬ mudlarks
Frank ⎭
Sal, a maid-of-all-work
Maggie ⎫
Jack ⎬ crossing sweepers
Goose ⎭
Muvver, a coster girl
Coster 1 *
Coster 2 *
Coster 3 *
Bootlace Seller
Gingerbread Seller*
Soup Seller *
Peg, a lodging-house deputy
Sir Henry, a street reciter
Liza, a street-walker
Mrs Saunders (non-speaking)
May King
May Queen
Jack-in-the-Green
Costers, Chimney Sweeps, Passers-by

*Can be played as male or female

SYNOPSIS OF SCENES

The action takes place in and around Wapping, London

Time—mid nineteenth century

AUTHOR'S NOTE

The source material for the daily lives of the characters in *Dark River* comes from *London Labour and the London Poor* by Henry Mayhew, who was the father of Descriptive Sociology and Mass Observation, and who also provided inspiration for Charles Dickens. Their collective writing did much to improve the conditions of the poor in the second half of the nineteenth century.

Alexa Romanes

PRODUCTION NOTES

Staging

This play can be staged very simply, but ideally there should be plenty of space for movement in the acting area, with the audience arranged as close to the action as possible. The original production was designed as a thrust performance with the audience on three sides. A floor cloth on the rectangle surrounded by the audience represented the riverbed, the street crossing, etc. Upstage was a long rostrum from left to right with steps left and right and a central ramp. This area was used for the lodging-house as well as the street and the river-bank.

Costume should be mid nineteenth-century and realistically drab and ragged except for characters such as Sal, Liza and Sir Henry. Sal can seem to get grubbier in Act II by the addition of a filthier apron and messed-up hair. She will need assistance with her quick change before the last scene.

Casting

The age-range is 11 to 16, for speaking parts. Younger children can be included as sweeps and urchins. Roles that can be played as male or female are indicated in the cast list. If a smaller cast is required, the following parts can be doubled.

King/Soup Seller
Sir Henry /Whippet
Maggie/Coster
Liza /Coster
Goose/May King
Plug/Bootlace Seller /Jack-in-the-Green
Peg /Coster/May Queen
Jericho/Muvver
Jack/Gingerbread Seller

Music

The songs can be sung by all the cast. The music is available from Samuel French Ltd. "Dark River" has lyrics by Alexa Romanes and music by Jane Lloyd. "Ratcliffe Highway", "Blow Away the Morning Dew" and "Old Joe Clark" (Sweeps' Dance) are traditional.

For the sweeps' dance, any instrument or combination of instruments can be used appropriate to the period, most likely being tin whistle and violin.

ACT I

SCENE 1

A street in Wapping

A pool of light reveals a heap of rubbish and a pile of dirty sacks. Mouse sits by the heap. Sal is hidden beneath the pile of sacks. There are the sound effects of carriage wheels, horses and footsteps. Mouse is begging from passers-by (who can be real or imaginary according to numbers of cast available). She pauses, overcome by a racking cough

King strolls on with his gang: Jericho, Whippet and Plug. Mouse cowers, trying not to be noticed. The sound effects fade and the Lights come up to full

King What have we here, lads? I do believe it's a mudlark. A dirty, stinking little mudlark. What's your name?

Mouse curls into a ball. King kicks her

I said, what's your name?

Mouse doesn't answer

Jericho It's the one they call Mouse. She don't talk much.

King kicks her again and Mouse cries out

Whippet Nah, she only squeaks — 'cos she's a mouse!

The gang laugh

King So why aren't you mud-grubbing then, Mouse? It's low tide.

Mouse still doesn't speak. King nods to Plug who hauls her to her feet and propels her towards King

Plug The King don't like to say everything twice, Mouse. It spoils his temper.
King So — why aren't you at the river?
Mouse (*coughing*) I ain't very well.
King Ain't that a shame?

King nods at Plug, who lets her go

Jericho Just what we need, eh, King? She looks real pathetical.
King You read my very thoughts, Jericho. She'll make a first-rate decoy. Pity she's so very dirty.
Jericho We could clean her up a bit.
Whippet I ain't touching her!
Jericho Stick her in the horse-trough by *The Jolly Sailor*.

Mouse tries to make a dash for it but Plug grabs her again

King Good thinking, Jericho. Coughing and soaking wet. That should touch the ladies' hearts.
Mouse (*struggling*) I got to stay 'ere. I'm minding Annie's findings. She'll kill me if I leave 'em.
King And I'll kill you if you don't. Whippet, give Plug a hand. Hold her still. I want her to listen. Are you listening to me, Mouse? ... Are you?

Mouse nods

We're going up the 'Aymarket, where the theatres is. All you got to do, when the fine ladies and gents come by, is to stick out your grubby paw, squeak a bit ...
Jericho And look pathetical.
King And look pathetical.
Whippet While we whips their snitchwipers and purses.
King Stow it, Whippet. What she don't know, she can't tell. Let's be off then.
Jericho *The Jolly Sailor* first. And the water-trough!

Laughing, the gang is about to drag Mouse off. She starts to cry

Annie enters, carrying a broken basket

Annie Oi! What do you think you're doing? Let her go! Oh ... it's you. (*Ironically*) The King. I might have known. Leave her alone.
King Mind your own business, Annie. I got a job for her.
Annie Leave her be. She's looking after my haul.

Nobody moves

Leave her be, King, or it'll be the worse for you. I can lay information against you, any time I like. You see, last November, the fourteenth I think it was, I jist 'appened to be in Gissing's gin-shop. Dressed very swell you was. And I saw you pass a bad note. And that's a hanging offence, that is. And wouldn't I like to see you swing!

King (*unnerved, but covering it*) I doubt if you'll have that pleasure, my dear. After all, who is going to believe the likes of you?

Mouse has been crying and now lets out a wail

(*Becoming irritated*) Oh, let her go. She wouldn't be no good anyway. A wash wouldn't make no difference. Filth goes right down to the bone with a mudlark. Leave her, Plug. We got other fish to fry.

Plug, Whippet and Jericho start to drift off

King moves close to Annie

(*Quietly*) I shan't forget this, Annie. You think you got one over me, but you're wrong. Very wrong.

King pats her on the cheek — then ostentatiously wipes his hand on a handkerchief. He exits with the rest of the gang

Annie Are you all right, Mouse? Come here.

They sit down. Annie puts her arm round Mouse who is coughing again

That cough's worse. (*Feeling her forehead*) No fever, that's good.
Mouse I'm cold. And I can't feel me feet no more.
Annie We got to get you some boots somehow. I found a lot of coal today, down by them Dutch barges. With yesterday's haul, that's a potful. I'll get a penny for that. (*She starts to scrabble in the pile of junk*) There must be nearly six pounds of bones here, that's another tuppence, and I got a good length of rope somewhere.

Suddenly Annie stands up and puts a finger to her lips to warn Mouse. She points to the heap of sacks

I got a good haul here. You done well, Mouse, looking after it all ...

Annie pulls off the pile of sacking, revealing Sal. Despite a night in the open, Sal looks better dressed and cleaner than the mudlarks. She is confused and frightened. Mouse is backing off, ready to run, but Annie remains calm

It's all right, Mouse. She don't look dangerous.

Sal re-arranges her shawl and puts on her bonnet as she gets up. During the following, she keeps looking around as if she's frightened

What were you doing, hiding under my findings?

Sal I were trying to keep warm, like. I bin here all night. I think I fell asleep. I don't know where I am.

Annie This is Wapping, back of Vinegar Lane. 'Ere, you don't 'alf talk funny. You ain't from round 'ere.

Sal No, I come from Hampshire.

Annie Where's that? Near Clapham?

Sal No. It's a long way away. It's the country.

Mouse What country?

Sal *The* country. Where there's fields, and woods, and cows and sheep ...

Mouse Have you got a river?

Sal Oh, yes. My village is right by a river.

Annie Bet it ain't as big as our river. Bet it ain't got barges and steamers and cargo ships.

Sal No, I haven't seen nothing as big as the Thames before.

Annie You ain't just come from the country though. Or if you did, you didn't walk. Your boots are clean.

Sal I left the village last summer, to be apprenticed as maid-of-all-work.

Annie Where?

Pause

You were thrown out, weren't you? You're out of a place.

Sal You ask a lot of questions.

Annie Sorry. I'm Annie, by the way. And this is Mouse.

Mouse is fingering Sal's shawl in admiration

Leave her be, Mouse. You'll make her dirty.

Sal I'm Sal.

They eye one another

Why are you so muddy?

Annie 'Cos we're mudlarks.

Sal Larks? That sounds fun.

Annie Fun! You don't know nothing, do you? Wading about in the river mud every low tide with bare legs, winter as well. Bent in two, scrabbling about with your hands in the filth ...

Sal But why?

Annie For the findings, of course. Coal dropped from the barges, bits of old iron, rope, bones, copper nails out of the ships lying along shore — they're the best, fourpence a pound we can get for those, but it's difficult to get so many. The crews drive us away if they see us. At night, when it's low tide, some of the big lads go with a claw to pull the nails out, or they climb into the coal barges for the sweepings. Course, that's stealing, that is, and Mouse's brother got seven days in the House of Correction for that.

Mouse 'E said it were wonderful.

Sal Wonderful?

Mouse 'E 'ad a coat, shoes *and* stockings given him, and the food was regular.

Pause while Annie assesses Sal

Annie Well, your rig is good enough for you to get another job, no trouble. You don't want to go on sleeping in the streets, you'll soon go downhill. I'd give anything to go into service, me, but no chance, looking like this. And I'll never earn enough for better clothes.

Sal I'm not going back into service. She'll find me.

Annie Oh that's it, is it? You run away? Was the missus cruel then — or did you pinch something?

Sal I never took anything in my life!

Annie No, course you didn't. Don't go. Look, I can help you. Show you the best lodging-house, help you find your way about, get you a job — no, not mudlarking, something better than that ...

Sal I can look after myself, thank you very much. I don't need your help.

Sal marches off

Annie Come back! (*She sighs and shakes her head*) Me and my big mouth. She's got no more idea than a baby. And she's really frightened of something, did you notice that? Kept looking around all the time. The sharks'll see her coming a mile off. Oh well, I'd better get this stuff to the rag shop. Give us a hand, Mouse, and you can share my dinner.

Annie and Mouse carry off the sacks, etc.

The traffic sound effects of carriage wheels, horses, etc. fade up for the next scene

SCENE 2

The street crossing

The sound effects fade down a little behind the following speech. The sound effects should continue at low level throughout this scene

Maggie enters into a spotlight, Jack enters in the shadows. Both carry brooms. Maggie regards the imaginary bustling scene with relish

Maggie Wapping High Street on a Saturday afternoon — all noise and bustle. Carts rattling to and fro from St Katherine's Dock. Carriages and hansom cabs. The omnibus from Shadwell to Whitechapel — all in a tearing hurry. Jingle of harness, crack of whips, and a stream of ripe curses. Unlucky dockers, not hired today, drag themselves to the nearest pub, a gang of shouting sailors making for the same destination. Housewives lug their baskets of provisions with bowed shoulders and emigrants on their way to the quay drag their trunks and bundles over the cobbles. Look — there's a Customs-House officer in his brass-buttoned jacket. And there's a black bosun in a silk waistcoat with a red handkerchief twisted round his head like a turban. He's arguing with another old salt with a greasy pigtail, a brass earring and a monkey shivering on his shoulder. (*She sniffs the air*) I can smell the fumes of tobacco and rum from the warehouses — strong enough to mask the stink of the refuse and the horse-manure. (*Cheerily lifting her broom*) But if it weren't for the dirt and the dung — we wouldn't be here! Come on, Jack, on yer toes!

The Lights come up as Maggie and Jack take up positions either side of the street. The sound effects come up during the sweeping sequences. The passers-by can be real or imaginary

Jack Two gents and a doll!

Two men and a woman cross

Jack sweeps energetically across the street, then touches his cap and holds out his hand

Thank you, sir! ... A fourpenny piece! How about that, Maggie? I ain't had one o' them before.
Maggie (*casually*) I got a tanner from a toff yesterday — (*Catching sight of a customer*) My gent!

A man crosses

She sweeps across the street. Jack is cross at having missed him. While Maggie collects her money and bobs a curtsy, Jack spies customers on Maggie's side of the street and runs across to them

Jack A gentleman and a doll! Mine!

Maggie And a child! They're mine!

A man, a woman and a child cross

Jack and Maggie sweep furiously across the road and hold their hands out. Only Jack gets anything

Sal enters and hovers on the opposite side of the street

You didn't call the child. They were mine, you little toad.
Jack 'E only give me a farthing.
Maggie That's not the point, Jack. It's the rules. I'll tell Goose. (*Seeing Sal*) A doll! Mine!

Maggie crosses to Sal who has plucked up the courage to cross the busy road. Maggie holds her back

Mind the carriage! You were nearly a goner then.

Maggie sweeps Sal across, then holds out her hand

Sal I'm sorry. I haven't got any money.
Maggie I didn't think you would have, somehow. In service, are you?
Sal Not any more. Look, I need to earn some money, real quick. I haven't had nothing to eat since the day before yesterday.

Maggie and Jack look at Sal suspiciously and then at one another

Goose enters on the opposite side of the street

I mean, I wondered if I could do what you're doing — sweep the crossing. It don't look too difficult.
Jack No, you can't. This is Goose's patch. You have to belong to his gang. So sling your hook.
Maggie 'Ang on, Jack. Look, you can see she's faint with hunger. (*Seeing Goose*) Let's see what Goose says. Oi! Goose!

Goose crosses the road to join them. He has a slight stammer and a gentle manner

Sal (*whispering*) Why is it his gang? You're older than he is.
Maggie 'E was on this crossing first, and 'e makes the rules ... Goose, this girl 'ere wants to join us.

Goose A dollymop? Does she now. W-w-what makes you w-want to do that?

Sal I'm out of a place, if you please, sir.

Goose Sir! (*He laughs*) You can call me Goose.

Sal That's a strange name.

Goose I w-were christened Tom Gander, so it's Goose. See?

Maggie Goose is our captain. 'E looks out for us — there are six of us altogether. And if someone ain't doing so well, he gives 'em some of his own money to tide 'em over.

Jack Goose earns the most of us all, 'cos 'e can tumble and that. You should see 'im. Cartwheels, backflips and all sorts.

Goose W-when it's dry I tumbles after the omnibuses and p-people throw p-pennies from the top deck. At night I goes up the Strand or the 'Aymarket and tumbles when folk come out of the theatres. They're generally in a good mood and the gents w-want to look flash in front of the ladies, so they're free with their cash.

Maggie A toff give 'im a half-sovereign once, didn't 'e, Goose? When you done twenty head-over-heels all in a row outside the theatre.

Goose suddenly upends himself and walks on his hands

Goose You catch 'em una-w-wares and then they laugh. And if they laugh, you got 'em. Though some bright sparks think it more fun to trip you up with their w-walking sticks.

Goose stands up. The others clap and he bows

Sal I can't do that.

Maggie You don't have to. Just sweep, and be respectful. And watch out for the traffic.

Jack And if you see the peelers, you run.

Goose Or if one of the gang is around, give them the money, and they'll r-run. It ain't a crime to sweep the streets, just to take money for it. We all meet at our lodging house later and share the money out again.

Jack She ain't got a broom. Tuppence ha'penny they cost from the old woman in Bridge Street.

Maggie Look, I'll go down the baker's shop and get us a pennyworth of bread. She can 'ave my broom while I'm gone, and see how she gets on.

Jack Goose 'asn't said as she can yet.

They all look at Goose

Goose She can have a go. Sort of a trial. But you got to obey the rules. W-what's yer name?

Sal Sal. What are the rules?

Goose If there's more than w-one of yer on the same crossing, yer 'ave to call.

Sal Call?

Jack If yer see someone coming to cross the road — say it's a lady and a gentleman, whoever calls out first "a doll and a gent", sweeps for 'em and gets the money.

Maggie (*with a look at Jack*) But if you call out wrong — say there were really three of 'em, the other sweeper can call out right, and they belong to her.

Sal Oh, *that* was what you were doing. I see.

Maggie Right. I'm off to get us something to eat, before you peg out. Here's the broom. Look after it — and don't get run over.

Maggie exits

Goose And remember the rules!

Goose cartwheels off

Jack gives Sal a push. The traffic sound effects fade up again

Jack You go the other side.

Sal dodges nervously over the road and takes up her position

A Passer-by enters behind Sal

Sal doesn't see him. Jack does and dashes over the road

A gent! Mine! You gotta be quicker than that!

Sal spots a group of Passers-by on Jack's side, but he is too quick for her

Two men with two women come and go

Two gents, two dolls! ... Thank you, sir, thank you, lady.

Jack sees someone in the distance

There's a peeler coming down the street! ... Don't just stand there — it's a policeman, you ninny! Quick, take my money — go on, take it — and run! *Run!*

Jack gives Sal a shove

Sal runs off

He stands with his broom, whistling nonchalantly as a whistle blows and the Lights and sound effects fade

Song: Dark River

Oh London's a fine place, if you make your way.
She'll show you her kind face if you earn good pay.
But if you are poor and you ain't got some work,
You belong to the cold fog, the mud and the dirt.

Dark river, dark river, that flows to the sea.
One day take me with you, and let me be free.

Invisible children in rags and bare feet,
Our father's the river, our mother's the street.
Hard blows for a teacher and hunger for nurse,
Our playmate is fear and our names are a curse.

Dark river, dark river, that flows to the sea,
One day take me with you and let me be free.

SCENE 3

The river

The acting area is strewn with pieces of mud-caked metal, bone, rope, etc.

There are river sound effects and a rippling light comes up on Annie, Mouse and Frank working. They each have a filthy container into which they put objects as they find them. The mudlarks cannot see them until they have felt for them and pulled them out of the mud, during the course of the action. They move slowly, and with difficulty, occasionally straightening up to relieve their aching backs. Mouse is coughing and shivering with cold

Annie It's an east wind, Mouse, that's why it's a cutting one. I can smell salt. That's the sea. Wouldn't it be grand to get on one of them steamers, and go all the way down the river to the sea?

They continue to work

Sal runs on to the bank. She is panting and has a stitch. It takes her a while to recover. Then she waves at Annie

Sal Annie! Annie! ... Over here! It's me — Sal!

Annie looks up and begins to wade towards her

Annie Oh, it's you. I'm glad you come back.
Sal I need your help. I don't know what to do. I got all this money, and I don't know what to do with it.
Annie 'Ang on a mo. (*She gathers up her haul and pulls herself up on to the steps*) The tide's coming in. We'll have to stop soon, anyway.
Sal (*flinching away from her*) It's awful ... it's awful!
Annie What is?
Sal What you do. There in the mud. That boy's up to his waist in it. And look at you — you look like — I don't know — like something dragged up from the bottom of our village pond.
Annie That's nice! And you just said you needed my help an' all!
Sal I'm sorry, I didn't mean ——
Annie Anyway, I can think of worse jobs. Chimney sweep, sewer-hunter, collecting dog turds for the tannery. And I wouldn't do what Frank's sister does for any kind of money.

Frank and Mouse are climbing the steps

Frank What's that about my sister?
Annie Nothing.

Frank and Mouse sit on the steps and pick over their findings

Now, Sal, you were shouting out something about some money.
Sal Oh — yes. I met some kids who were sweeping a crossing. Goose and his gang ...
Annie Know 'em well.
Frank Goose is a good sort.
Sal The girl ...
Annie Maggie, that would be.
Sal She lent me her broom. And then she went off and left me with this boy — curly hair he had ...
Frank That's Jack.

Sal I think that was his name — anyway, I didn't earn any money, 'cos Jack was so much quicker than me, and then this policeman came along and Jack gave me all his money and told me to run. I ran and I ran, I was so frightened of being taken up by the police, only I got lost and couldn't find my way back to the crossing. And I've still got Maggie's broom. She'll think I've pinched it.

Frank She will an' all! Won't she be in a temper!

Annie And Jack'll think you've run off with his money. My, you're in trouble.

Sal (*breaking down*) And I'm in such trouble already.

Mouse Don't cry. Annie'll think of something. She's clever. She's bin to school.

Annie Only to the ragged school for a while, when I was little, when me parents was alive. They never even learned me to read, and I was there three whole weeks. Anyway, it's simple. We'll find Maggie and Jack at Ma Grogan's lodging-house. They always go to the same one. And I got enough findings here so we can all have a roof over our heads tonight. No doorways for us. And before that, we'll go to the Saturday night market for something to fill our bellies. The rag-shop first, to get our money.

Frank I'll come with yer. Thought I ain't got much today.

Annie Why are you limping, Frank?

Frank Cut me foot on a bit of glass.

Taking their findings with them, they are moving off

Annie You want to get that seen to. It'll go bad.

Frank Don't fuss — it don't hurt half as much as me chilblains, and I've 'ad them all winter.

Sal and the Mudlarks exit

The river sound effects crossfade to market effects for the next scene

SCENE 4

The market

There are sounds of carts, barking dogs, loud talk, a hurdy-gurdy, etc.

The Lights come up on the Costers who are calling out their wares in fierce competition with one another. Repeat their cries until scene is established. The Costers carry large baskets, the Bootlace Seller and Gingerbread Seller carry trays with straps around their necks and the Soup Seller pushes a small cart with pot, ladle and bowls

Coster 1 Three a penny, Yarmouth bloaters! Come and look at 'em! Here's toasters!

Bootlace Seller Pick 'em out cheap here! Four pair a ha'penny, bootlaces!

Muvver Apples eight a penny — fine russets!

Coster 2 Penny a bunch — *here's* your turnips!

Coster 3 Fresh watercress. Two bunches a ha'penny!

Gingerbread Seller Hot spiced gingerbread! Hot spiced gingerbread! Buy my gingerbread, sm-o-o-o-king hot!

Soup Seller Ha'penny a half-pint, ha'penny a half-pint! Piping-hot pea soup! Come and try it!

The Costers move in turn into the spotlight. The sound effects fade

Coster 1 Saturday night. Pay-time! A few brief moments to savour the clink of coins in yer pocket. And there's Sunday dinner to be bought. It's more of a fair than a market. The streets are near impassable with the jostling crowds. There are hundreds of stalls, and every stall has its white glare of the gas lamp or else the red smoky flame of the old-fashioned grease lamp. There's the crimson of the fire shining through the holes of the roast chestnut stove. Then there's the sparkle from the glass globes of the grocer's shops, and the butcher's gaslights streaming and fluttering in the wind, like flags of flame. The whole market looks as if it's on fire.

Bootlace Seller The traffic of carts and carriages in the nearby main street is drowned by the eager cries of the coster-mongers and dealers, all shouting at the tops of their voices. It's a head-splitting racket. Do yer know, the number of older costers with no voice at all is phenomenal! They 'as to get boys to shout for 'em. Our higher voices cut through the din, see?

Muvver Adding to the racket is the drone of the blind beggar, drowned by the shrill tooting of the penny-whistle player, the butcher sharpening his knives, the down-at-heel preacher thundering hell-fire and perdition as he waves his tracts, unheeded. More popular is the trio of ballad singers on the corner of the street, competing with jingling music of the barrel organ across the way. And outside the penny concert hall, a man in a battered top hat and a violent waistcoat is urging the passer-by to "Be in time! Be in time! Mr Gallimandi is about to sing that popular ditty, 'The Knife Grinder'!"

Coster 2 The sights are as bewildering as the sounds. Here's a stall glittering with new saucepans, there another, bright with blue and yellow crockery and sparkling with white glass. Now you come to a row of old shoes arranged along the kerb, then to a stand of gaudy tea-trays, next to a stall with red handkerchiefs and blue shirts flapping back and forth from a line stretched across the pavement.

Coster 3 This stall is green and white with bunches of turnips, that one red with apples, the next yellow with onions, and another purple with pickling cabbages. Little boys of six or seven wriggle their way through the press of people, holding up three or four beetroot like a posy, whining for custom.

Gingerbread Seller There's mongrel dogs of all shapes and sizes, yelping as they are trodden underfoot, barking in contest with the barrel organ and with one another, and generally keeping a beady eye on the forbidden glories of the butcher's shop and the hot pie stand. There are children everywhere. More are selling than buying, but a gaggle of them has gathered round the peep-show of The Death of Nelson. They are paying with bottles rather than money, to the disappointment of the showman. Next to this cheery crowd stand a more forlorn group of youngsters with their parents. They are begging, the mother with a baby at her ragged breast, the father with his head down, as if in shame.

Soup Seller Until you see it, hear it, smell it, you can have no idea of the scramble that is going on to make a living, the determined struggle for a few grimy copper coins to pass from one toil-worn hand to another.

The market sound effects fade up and calls of the Costers start again

Sal, Annie, Mouse and Frank enter, with hunks of bread, which they are eating ravenously. Other Children enter during the following to buy from the Costers. Whippet also enters (with Plug and Jericho if they are not doubling as Costers). He is planning some thieving. We see him pinch an apple, unnoticed, before turning his attention to the Bootlace Seller. The market sound effects fade to a low level

Annie Soup! Come on, my treat. We can share two half-pints. ... What's the matter, Sal?

Sal I thought I saw someone ... It's all right. They've gone I think. Perhaps I imagined it.

Annie You're as nervous as a cat. You need a bit more inside you, you do. (*To the Soup Seller*) Two half-pints o' pea-water, please.

Frank and Mouse hoot with laughter. The Soup Seller is not amused

Soup Seller Show us yer money first, you dirty little tyke.

Annie waves a penny under his nose. He pockets it and serves the soup

Annie This'll warm us all up.

She passes a bowl to Sal to share. The Soup Seller holds out the other bowl to Mouse but Frank intercepts it and downs his share in a few gulps. Mouse tugs at his sleeve until he reluctantly passes the bowl to her

Frank I'm going to see if I can find a pair of boots.

Frank limps off

Annie takes the bowl from Sal

Annie The tight little bastard! Not enough money for bread and soup, but enough stashed away for a pair o'boots. (*A bitter laugh*) 'E'll go a long way, that one. Frank'll pull himself out of the mud all right.
Sal So will you, Annie. You won't be a mudlark all your life.
Annie Won't I? There's plenty as are ... No, I don't think I'll ever leave the river. Can't hang on to my money, that's the trouble. Talking of which, have you got Jack's safe?
Sal Yes.
Annie Well, keep your hand over your pocket and watch out if anyone jostles yer. Saturday night is terrible for pickpockets. Mouse, you keep look-out for us. You know all the dippers and dodgers.
Muvver Fine russets! Eight a penny! ... Hallo, Annie. How you doin'? Evening, Mouse. And who's this?
Annie This is our new friend, Sal. Sal, this is Muvver.
Sal She can't be your mother, Annie! She's our age!
Annie Course not, stupid! All the kids round 'ere call 'er Muvver, 'cos she's kind to us. Best of all the coster girls, is Muvver.
Muvver Get away with you, Annie. 'Ere, 'ave an apple. Go on, 'ave one each. I'm down to the bottom of the basket, and they're a bit wrinkled, mind.

Frank enters with a pair of old boots. He moves towards the Bootlace Seller

Sal Thank you, Muvver.
Muvver Polite, ain't she?
Annie She's from the country. And she's been in service.

A commotion breaks out around the Bootlace Seller

Bootlace Seller Gotcha, yer little thief!
Frank What, me? No, I ain't pinched nothing.
Bootlace Seller You snaffled a bunch of my bootlaces.
Frank No I never. It weren't me.
Bootlace Seller Spent all your money on the boots, so thought you'd have some laces for free, eh?
Frank Let me go. It weren't me and I'll prove it. I'll fight yer.
Coster 1 A fight! A fight!

Other Costers take up the call and everyone gathers round. The Bootlace
Seller takes off his jacket and scarf. Annie takes Frank aside

Annie What's going on, Frank?
Frank This cove said I pinched some bootlaces, but I never.
Annie Didn't you.
Frank No, honest. But I saw who did. It was Whippet.
Sal Why didn't you say?
Frank King'd 'ave my guts for garters!
Coster 1 (*to the Bootlace Seller*) You teach him a lesson, Bert! (*To Coster*
2) Our Bert knows 'ow to work his fists well. He could muzzle half a dozen
bobbies before breakfast.
Sal Muvver, can't you stop them fighting?
Muvver No, luv. If you stop a fight it causes bad blood for life. If they fight,
they shake hands after, and then forget all about it.
Sal But Frank'll get hurt. He's much smaller than the other lad. Why didn't
he call a policeman if he really thinks Frank stole something?
Muvver Policeman! If there's one thing us costers hate worse than a thief
it's a peeler! No, you let 'em settle it their own way.

The crowd have formed a circle. The Costers and other sellers supporting the
Bootlace Seller (Bert), a few ragged children are backing Frank with Annie,
Sal and Mouse. Frank has now taken off his shirt and the two boys are
squaring up to each other. The Soup Seller takes on the role of referee

Soup Seller Now, lads, no kicking, no wrestling and no punches below the
belt. First one to give the other a good noser is the winner. Ready? One, two,
three!

The Soup Seller drops his hanky and Frank and the Bootlace Seller begin to
spar, the crowd yelling encouragement. After a while, Frank begins to lose
his temper and swings wildly. The Bootlace Seller lands him one on the nose.
The Soup Seller tries to declare him the winner, but Frank launches himself
on his adversary, butting him in the stomach and knocking him over. Annie
tries to drag Frank off, the Soup Seller tries to intervene, but is attacked by
one of the urchins and everyone is drawn into a general mêlée — except
Mouse who crouches by the abandoned tray of gingerbread and begins to
stuff her mouth and pockets. At the climax of the fight, there is the sound of
a police whistle, followed by cries of "Peelers!", etc.

Gradually the fighters detach themselves from the fray and run off,
gathering up belongings as they go

Annie collects Sal and Mouse then turns back to drag off Frank

Bootlace Seller (*as he goes*) I won fair and square, you cheat!
Annie Come away, Frank! The peelers are coming, Quick! Run!

They run off to distant shouts and whistles

*The sound of the hurdy-gurdy music fades up. Black-out. The music fades.
The clock strikes twelve under the sound of rain*

SCENE 5

The lodging-house

There is the sound of rain. A spot comes up on Sal. She still has the broom

Sal Ma Grogan's lodging-house, right by the dark river. Rat's Castle, Annie
calls it. Looks like a prison. Soot-black walls, bars on the basement
windows, the upper ones broken and stuffed with paper and rags. I don't
want to go in, but it's cold and raining and Annie's already banging on the
door.

The Lights come up on Annie and Mouse

Sal joins them and the spot fades

Annie Open up! Open up!
Peg (*off*) All right! All right! I'm coming.

*Peg enters with a candle. Although better dressed than the mudlarks, she
is an unattractive girl who has the hunched shuffle of an old woman and
a permanent cold*

Oh, it's you.
Annie Where's Ma Grogan, Peg?
Peg Out. I'm her deputy tonight. And we're full. Top to tail like kippers on
all three floors. (*She yawns*)
Sal Let's go somewhere else.
Mouse (*coughing*) I can't go no further, Annie.
Annie We got to get in here, Sal. This is where Jack and Goose'll be. You
got to get the money back to them, remember? ... Can't you fit us in
somewhere, Peg? We've got the money.

Peg The kids are in the cellar tonight, if you're looking for Goose's gang. Only thing is, the sewer water could be rising, with all this rain. Oh, and King and his lot are in there an' all. (*She sniffs and wipes her nose on her sleeve*)
Annie We'll risk it. Let us in.

Peg leads the way into the cellar

The Lights come up on King, Jericho and Plug playing cards. Goose, Maggie and Jack are trying to sleep. Other children huddle under dirty blankets and sacking, or sit on stools talking quietly

Peg (*indicating some mattresses and blankets*) There are some shake-downs over there. And Ma Grogan says I'm to take the money first.
Annie Here you are. Frank'll be along soon, I expect — but 'e can pay for 'imself.
Peg Ta. I 'ope madam sleeps well. And if you want anything — don't call me.

Peg shuffles off, yawning

Annie Give us one of your boots, Sal.
Sal What?
Annie Yer boot. Go on, quick!

Sal quickly slips off a boot and hands it to Annie who goes to a vacant mattress, throws off the blanket, then attacks the mattress with the boot

Gotcha, yer varmints! (*She holds out the boot to Sal*) Go on. You better do your mattress. The place is crawling with bugs.

Sal takes back the boot and squeamishly thumps her mattress. The girls shake out their blankets and try to make themselves comfortable. Mouse goes to sleep quickly

King (*putting down a winning card and gathering up coins*) My game, I think.
Plug (*admiringly*) 'Ow do you do it, King? I 'ad a good hand then, and you still came out best.
King Skill and concentration, old son.
Jericho (*muttering*) And playing with yer own cards.
King What was that you said, Jericho?
Jericho I said you was always lucky at cards, King.
Sal What's that over there in the shadows? I saw something move. It's a rat!

Annie (*with a laugh*) Only one?

Sal sees the rat move again, and screams. The sleepers wake up

Maggie Shut that noise! I need my sleep.
Goose W-what's going on?
Jack It's 'er! That's the one! That's the dollymop who took my money!

The Sweepers get up and surround Sal

Maggie Yeah, that's 'er. I'd know that bonnet and shawl anywhere.
Goose B-breaking the rules, eh?
Sal I didn't mean to take Jack's money. He gave it to me to look after.
Goose W-why didn't you b-bring it b-back when the coast w-was clear?
Sal I got lost. I couldn't find any of you.

The Sweepers look disbelieving

Maggie Pull the other leg, it's got a bell on! And to think I was helping yer.
    And where's my broom, eh? You pinched that too.
Sal It's here. And I've got all the money safe.
Jack I bet you 'ave. Give it to me!

Sal gives Jack the money and he starts counting it

Annie She's telling the truth, Goose. She really did get lost. She don't know
    the streets like we do. I brought her here special so she could find you and
    give the money back.
Goose Is all the money there, Jack?

Jack has counted the money. He nods

I b-believe you then. And if Annie v-vouches for you ...
Annie I do.
Goose Then there's no more to be said.

Peg and Frank enter

Peg 'Ere they all are. Room for one more skinny 'un. Pay up first. Ma's
orders.

Frank hands over the money and goes into the cellar

Peg exits

King Frank, me old friend! Have you done that little service for me?

Frank hands over a bottle

And the change?

Frank reluctantly hands it over

Frank Don't I get nothing for my trouble?
King You get my thanks, Frankie. (*He takes a swig from the bottle*) And even better than that, I promise not to give you a cuff round the ear for your impudence.

Jericho and Plug laugh

Frank Laugh away. I know something that'll wipe the smile from your faces.

Everyone looks at Frank

Whippet's bin taken up by the peelers.
Jericho Never! Whippet's too sharp for that!
Frank Not quite sharp enough. He's in Wapping clink right now, having been caught with a quantity of bootlaces — (*he looks triumphantly at Annie*) — and some bad coins. ... Now I wonder where he got them from, eh?

Plug and Jericho gather round King and they whisper together anxiously

Annie (*to Frank*) What you bin up to? You didn't peach on Whippet, did you? King'll kill you.

Peg and Sir Henry enter. Sir Henry is dressed as a theatrical gentleman complete with necktie, battered top hat and cane. The clothes are a little shabby, but he is cleaner and more flamboyant than the rest of the children. His voice is resonant and his gestures dramatic

Peg You don't want to go in the cellar, Sir Henry. It's stinking damp. I can find some room for you on the top floor. You wouldn't have to share, not with too many.
Sir Henry I have not had a good day, Peg my dear. I'm afraid the cellar it will have to be. Take my miserable penny, you charming creature.
Peg (*simpering*) Ooh, Sir Henry! You are a card and no mistake!

Sir Henry gives her an elaborate bow

Peg giggles and exits

Sir Henry enters the cellar, looks about him and sighs theatrically. A child who has been sitting on a stool, vacates it for him. He sits to remove his shoes and shake water out of them

Sal (*astounded*) Who is that?!
Annie That is Sir Henry. He's a Street Reciter.
Maggie (*adoringly*) Isn't 'e lovely? Don't he dress nice!
Sal Is he a real lord, then?
Annie Don't be daft! 'E's an actor. 'E's too young to get much work in the theatre, so 'e performs in the streets and the pubs. 'E's pretty good, too.
Maggie Good? You should hear 'im! He does melodrama, poetry, Shakespeare and all that. 'E does a lovely Omlet.
Annie 'Amlet, Maggie.
Maggie Whatever. Do you think he'll do a piece for us tonight?
Annie I doubt it. 'E don't look in the mood.
Sir Henry (*watching the rats*) Hence vile rodent! (*He throws a shoe*) Hence!

Maggie dashes to retrieve the shoe and shyly returns it

Maggie 'Ere you are, Sir 'Enry. The rats are gone. You didn't 'alf give 'em a fright.
Sir Henry Maggie! My own dear Maggie, and how are you?
Maggie Oh, I'm all right ... 'Ere, let me 'elp you.

Maggie kneels to put his shoes back on

Sal (*aside to Annie*) She'd do well in service.
Annie (*shaking her head*) That's what love does to yer. Daft, innit?
Sir Henry And who else do we have residing at Grogan's Grand Hotel tonight? Goose and young Jack, I see.
Goose Evening, Sir Henry.
Sir Henry And King and his court. Sire, I salute you.

Sir Henry bows and King raises his bottle

King Cheers!
Sir Henry Ah, the formidable Annie. (*He bows*) The resourceful Frank.

Frank gives a mock salute. Sir Henry gently nudges the sleeping bundle that is Mouse with his foot. She wakes

And the invisible Mouse.

Mouse Sir Henry.
Sir Henry And who is this?
Sal (*bobbing a curtsy*) I'm Sal, m'lord.
Annie She's a friend of mine. She's all right.

Sir Henry kisses Sal's hand. Maggie is jealous and barges between them

Maggie I've shaken up a bed for you. There aren't no pillows left, but you can 'ave mine.
Sir Henry Thank you, Maggie, you're a treasure.
King (*aside to Plug and Jericho*) Just who does 'e think 'e is, the prancing Nancy!
Jericho 'E ought to know who's boss of this patch, King.
Plug I'll learn 'im for yer. Just say the word.
King There's too many of his friends around. Later. We'll see to 'im later.
Maggie Do us a recitation, Sir Henry.
Annie Oh yes! Give us a bit of Tragedy. I love all that jaw-breaking stuff.
Sal I never seen an actor before.
Sir Henry Ladies! Ladies! Have pity on a poor thespian! This very night I have given of my Macbeth, my Hamlet and my Othello at Drury Lane — to the waiting crowds outside the theatre. And I dare say it was better than anything they were likely to see inside the building. I am totally, but totally exhausted.

There is the sound of a heated argument off

Liza (*off*) Don't be so bloody ridiculous, Peg. Let me in!
Peg (*off*) Ma said you wasn't to stay here no more. Orders is orders.

Liza storms on, followed by Peg. She is flashily dressed and obviously made up

Liza Stay here? You think I'd want to stay in this flea-ridden, bug infested hell-hole? I just want to speak to my brother.
Peg (*sniffing*) He ain't here.
Liza For God's sake wipe yer nose, Peg — and don't bother fibbing. I know Frank's 'ere, 'cos I saw 'im come in.
Peg All right. But you're not stopping, so don't make yerself too comfortable.

Peg exits and Liza enters the cellar. Frank sees Liza immediately, and covers himself with a blanket to avoid being seen. Liza looks around. Some are asleep, others deliberately ignore her. Plug gives a wolf whistle, but is nudged by Jericho

King Evening, Liza. What brings you down our way? Business bad up the 'Aymarket?

Liza pulls a face at him and moves on

Annie Hallo, Liza.
Liza Annie. Seen Frank?

Annie nods in Frank's direction. Liza shakes him

Liza Wake up, Frank. It's me, Liza.
Frank Leave me alone. I told you I don't want to see you no more.
Liza Don't be silly. I brought you some money.
Frank I don't want your money. I got a living.
Liza (*trying to put money in his hand*) Mudlarking ain't a living. It's just another way of starving. Look at you! Look at your hands! You could grow mustard and cress on them. And yer feet, all cut to bits. If Mother were alive and could see you it would break her heart.
Frank You're the one who'd break her heart, Liza.
Liza For pity's sake, Frank! I couldn't stay a mudlark all my life. Think about it. There's old men and women out there on the river. We all know 'em. Bent double with age, still paddling and groping in the mud. They can't do nothing else. They don't know nothing else. I've got a chance to better myself. All right — I know it ain't what people would call "honest toil", but as soon as I've got enough money, I'll give it up, I promise.
Frank Liza! It's one of those things you can't leave off so easy, once you've took to it.
Liza Course I can. You'll see. I'll set myself up as a milliner, like Mother. And you can come and live with me, and go to school and learn a trade and 'ave a business of yer own.
Frank Dreams Liza, dreams! I don't need 'em. And I don't need your money.

He throws the money across the room. Pause. Everyone looks at the money, then at Liza and Frank

Liza marches out, head in air

Everyone looks at the money again. King nods at Plug who picks the money up and hands it to him. He pockets it

King What a charming domestic scene. A real piece of drama. Not quite your style, eh, Sir Henry? Now, perhaps we can all get some shut-eye.

Groans, moans and coughs as they all settle down, except for Sir Henry who appropriates the one candle and settles down to read the newspaper he has brought with him. Pause. Sal sits up, scratching madly. After a while she moves over to Sir Henry

Sal (*admiringly*) You can read ... I can only read a little bit, and write my own name and that. I went to our village school for a while, but then I had to leave. I were needed at home to help with the little ones. There are seven of us, and I'm the eldest. I do miss them — my brothers and sisters, although they were an awful plague to me at times. (*She starts to cry*)

Sir Henry Don't cry, Sal ... was that your name? Here, borrow my hanky.

Sal You're very kind. Everyone's been very kind, mostly. I'm just — just ... so afraid.

Sir Henry What are you afraid of?

Sal shakes her head and blows her nose

Look — shall I read you something, to take your mind off things?

Sal nods. Sir Henry looks through the paper

Yesterday's paper, I'm afraid. Stale news ... Ah, this looks interesting. "Horrid Murder in Rotherhithe."

Sal What! What did you say?

Sir Henry "Horrid Murder in Rotherhithe." Maybe not a good idea at this time of night. Might give you nightmares.

Sal No, go on, read it.

Sir Henry (*reading*) "There were distressing scenes early yesterday evening as the mutilated body of Mr Alfred Saunders, a forty-one-year-old bank clerk was found at his home at 17, Albion Terrace, Rotherhithe. The appalling discovery was made by a coalman making his regular delivery to the house. Before the coalman could run for assistance, the wife of the victim came upon the scene, having returned from a shopping trip to Whitechapel. Confronted by the sight of her husband's body, weltering in its gore, Mrs Saunders was overcome by hysteria and was led away by neighbours."

Gradually, during the reading, Annie, Maggie, King, Goose, Jack, Frank and the rest wake up and listen

(*Reading*) "It is apparent that the motive for this hideous crime was theft, as Mr Saunders' pocket-book was missing, and his desk and several cupboards in the house had been ransacked."

Sal No! No! That wasn't how it was!

Sir Henry (*reading*) "It is thought that Mr Saunders had been struck several blows with a heavy object over the back of the head as he sat in an armchair in the kitchen. Mrs Saunders was later able to make a statement to the police, in which she confirmed that money was missing ..."

Sal There was never any money in the house. That's why they were always quarrelling!

Sir Henry Do you know something about this?

Sal Go on! Go on! Read it!

Sir Henry (*reading*) "Mrs Saunders also informed them that since the murder, her maid-of-all-work, one Sally Newman, had disappeared. The maid knew where the household valuables were and Mrs Saunders had reason to doubt her honesty. Police are looking for her in connection with the murder and have issued the following description. Sally Newman is fourteen years of age, with fair hair and is of slim build and medium height. She speaks with a pronounced Hampshire accent and was probably wearing a paisley shawl and straw bonnet ..."

Sir Henry stops reading. All are focused on Sal

Annie Sal!

The others repeat her name as a whispered echo. Sal stands horror-struck. The Lights fade slowly to Black-out

ACT II

SCENE 1

The street in Wapping

The street is the same as Act I Scene 1. There is darkness and fog. There is a pool of light from a street lamp

King, Plug and Jericho creep on

King Jericho?
Jericho Yes, King?
King Over by the railings, Plug?
Plug Here, King.
King Stay by the corner and keep a good look out.

The clock strikes three

Look sharp now. Not a sound. And don't move unless I call yer.

Pause. Then a low whistle from Plug

Mrs Saunders enters, well muffled in a cloak and bonnet

King steps into the lamplight and casually puffing on a clay pipe. Mrs Saunders stays in the shadows throughout

You're the lady as was making enquiries in Gissing's gin-shop about a certain young party?

Mrs Saunders nods

So you got my message. Let's see the sovereign you promised, then …

Mrs Saunders doesn't move

Afraid to come into the light, are we? All right then.

King joins her in the shadows. She gives him a coin. King strolls back into the light

Well, the young person you was enquiring for frequents this part of the
river. At low-tide you'll find her grubbing with the mudlarks. Some nights
she'll be at Ma Grogan's lodging-house in Cinnamon Street. Other times
she'll be here in the streets between Wapping Stairs and St Katherine's
Dock. And sometimes she's with the sweepers at the crossing by the *Rose
and Crown*.

Mrs Saunders exits abruptly

Stupid bitch. I could've told her where the dollymop was right now, if she'd
waited.

Plug whistles

What?
Plug Sir Henry. Just come out of Hermit's Court.
King I told yer. Everything comes to those that wait.

Plug laughs as they crouch in the shadows

Sssssh!

Sir Henry crosses the street, humming a tune and swinging his cane

*At a signal from King, Plug and Jericho leap out from the shadows and knock
him down while King looks on*

His face! Give 'im a few in the face!

Plug and Jericho punch and kick Sir Henry

That'll do. Someone's coming!

King runs off, followed by Jericho and Plug

Sir Henry lies groaning

*Mouse runs on and nearly trips over him. She drops to her knees to see who
it is*

Mouse Annie! Annie! Over here!

Annie runs on

Annie Are we too late? Sorry, Sir Henry. We were trying to warn yer. We bin up the 'Aymarket looking for yer.

Sir Henry (*groaning*) My face, my face! How bad is it?

Annie Can't see. Let's get you into the light.

The girls help Sir Henry to the street lamp and sit him down. Annie takes out his handkerchief and dabs at his face

Sir Henry No broken teeth, thank God! — Ouch!

Annie Sorry. My word, you're gonna 'ave a real shiner in the morning.

Sir Henry (*taking a small mirror from a pocket and examining his face*) I won't be able to work for a week. And I have an audition tomorrow at the Victoria — for the part of the Long-Lost Heir in *The Castle of Fear*. A fine melodrama — a real part! They'll never have me, looking like this.

Annie King chose 'is moment, the bastard. He's got a down on me too, and I was frightened he'd peach on Sal to the peelers, just to get at me. A week's gone by, though, and 'e ain't done nothing yet.

Sir Henry And how is Sal? I don't suppose she took my advice?

Annie Nah. Too frightened to go the police 'erself. She reckons Mrs Saunders 'as got her story off pat, and'll put Sal's head in the noose if she can.

Mouse Fancy a lady being a murderer.

Sir Henry A bank clerk's wife is not a real lady, Mouse.

Mouse You know everything, you do, Sir Henry.

Sir Henry I do know that Sal is what they call a prime witness. She saw the whole thing after all.

Annie Saw the missus creep up behind 'im while 'e was asleep and smash 'is head in with the poker ... 'Orrible!

Sir Henry No wonder Sal is scared out of her wits.

Annie Yeah, she's convinced Mrs Saunders is going to find her and do 'er in, to stop her squealing. That is, if the peelers don't get to Sal first.

Sir Henry So she's lying low?

Annie Mostly at Ma Grogan's. She's there now, with Maggie. Look, it's only round the corner. Let's all go there and you can rest up.

Sir Henry What if King and his gang are there?

Annie They won't be. Ma Grogan's back and 'as banned them from the 'ouse. Says they give 'er lodgings a bad reputation' — if you can believe it!

They all start to laugh

Sir Henry Bad reputation? Not Ma Grogan's? ... Ow! I can't laugh. It hurts!

Annie and Mouse help Sir Henry off

The song "Ratcliffe Highway" is sung as the next scene is set for the lodging-house

Song: Ratcliffe Highway

As I was a-walking down London,
From Wapping to Ratcliffe Highway,
I chanced to pop into a gin-shop,
To spend a long night and day.

A doxy came rolling up to me,
And asked if I'd money to sport,
For a bottle of wine changed a guinea,
And this is the way I was caught.

When I asked for the change of my money,
She placed both her hands on her hip,
Saying "Sailor, now don't you be funny,
Do you think you're on board of your ship?"

But a gold watch hung over the mantel,
So the change for my guinea I take,
And down the stairs I run so nimbly,
Saying "Darn my old boots, I'm well paid."

So come all you bold young sailors,
That ramble down Ratcliffe Highway,
If you chance to pop into a gin-shop,
Beware lads how long you do stay.

SCENE 2

The lodging-house

The Lights come up on a convivial group — Sal, Maggie, Annie, Goose, Jack, Frank, Sir Henry, Peg and other urchins — singing and playing games such as cards, dice, knucklebones, etc. A bottle of beer is being passed round. Some have cups or mugs, others swig from the bottle. At the end of the song they break into chat in their various groups

Frank My idea of 'eaven. A pot o' beer and a quartern of gin after it, drunk neat. I can't abide water.

Annie We'd noticed. Inside or outside. When was the last time you 'ad a wash?

Frank Mind yer own business!

They start a friendly scuffle

Sir Henry You mustn't be so frightened, Sal. How could Mrs Saunders find you? It would be like looking for a needle in a haystack in this part of the city.

Sal You don't know her. She's the very devil. She never used to feed me proper. And she had eyes like a hawk. She just knew when I was thinking of creeping to the larder for a crust of bread ... You should have seen her face that day, when she turned, the poker in her hand all dripping with blood, you should have seen the look on her when she realized I was there at the scullery door. If I hadn't turned and bolted ...

Sal is shaking. Sir Henry puts an arm round her

It said in that paper of yours that there was money in the house. That was a lie for a start. They hadn't two farthings to rub together. They were always quarrelling about it. But he had an insurance on his life, see. I heard him say so when they were rowing about money. He'd say, never mind, you'll have plenty when I'm gone. To tease her, like. 'Cos, I mean, he were fit and healthy and not thinking of dying ...

They continue to talk in undertones

Maggie Oh, go on Goose. Let me try it. I'm sure it would earn us extra. Like the boys at the Vauxhall Bridge crossing. They sweep patterns and pictures in the mud. It makes people smile and then they give more money — specially the toffs. Look, I'll show you. Come on, Peg. Play the whistle for me. We bin practising, Goose. We can do it really well.

Maggie picks up two brooms and lays them in a cross on the floor. She positions herself and then nods to Peg who starts to play the whistle. The others gradually stop talking to watch. Maggie performs a broom dance

Music: The Keel Row (Broom Dance)

Applause from the others. Maggie looks to Sir Henry for approval

Sir Henry Charming, my dear, charming.

He blows her a kiss. Flushed with pride, Maggie turns to Goose

Goose I dunno, Mags. You do it very p-pretty. But are folk going to stop to w-watch you? Soon as they've crossed the road they're off.

Maggie Oh ... I suppose you're right, Goose. (*Pause*) 'Ow about I come with you of an evening when you go up the 'Aymarket? When you need a rest from yer tumbling an' that, I could do my dance.

Goose Maggie, I told yer before. The 'Aymarket at night ain't the place for a girl like you.

Maggie Why not?

Goose looks embarrassed

Annie It's where the doxies hang out, stupid. People might think you were one of them, now you've grown so tall.

Sir Henry And pretty.

Jack And besides, Goose and me 'ave other business to do and it wouldn't be right to 'ave you with us.

Maggie Why? What do you do?

Goose You're a blabbermouth, Jack.

Jack I ain't gonna tell 'er.

Maggie (*grabbing him*) Yes, you will!

Jack Ow! Let go!

Goose Let him go.

Maggie (*shaking him*) Tell me!

Jack No.

Goose Stop it, Maggie.

Maggie Tell me!

Annie I know what they do.

They stop and look at her

The toffs tip them to go and find girls for them, if they're too particular to trawl round the streets themselves. And the girls give 'em a bit of money too for bringing them where the gentlemen are waiting. Nice, eh?

Goose (*shrugging off his discomfort*) Supply and demand, Annie. We're doing a service, that's all.

Muvver enters

Peg 'Ere, who let you in?

Muvver Mrs Grogan.

Peg She still sober?

Muvver Just about.

Peg That's a miracle. You stopping?

Muvver What, 'ere? No thanks. I got a proper 'ome to go to. I've come to speak to Annie and Sal.

Annie At this time o' night?

Muvver It's nearly dawn, luv. I'm on my way to Covent Garden to get me apples. Look, I thought you should know that someone was asking for Sal around Wapping market.

Sal Who?

Muvver Tallish woman, in her thirties. Dressed genteel but shabby. Nice boots. Low voice, sharp nose. Couldn't see her eyes, because 'er bonnet was pulled right forward.

Sal That's her! That's her! I knew she'd find me!

Muvver Calm down. She 'asn't found you yet. Anyone who 'ad information was to leave a message at Gissing's gin-shop. Well, none of us costers'll be squealing. Everyone knows why you're on the run. We'll keep our mouths shut.

Annie See? Everyone's looking out for you, Sal. It'll be all right.

Muvver I just thought you should know. I got to go now. I 'ave to be at The Garden by five or all the best fruit is gone. See you.

Annie Thanks, Muvver.

Annie turns to comfort Sal

Muvver passes Liza coming in as she exits

Peg (*incredulous*) Ma Grogan never let you in?

Liza She's asleep and snoring in the passage-way.

Peg O Lor', I better take over.

Peg drags herself out. Liza moves to Frank

Liza I don't know why I've come back 'ere, after the last time.

Frank You shouldn't 'ave bothered.

Liza You're my brother, Frank. I care about you. I worry about you. I think about the river all the time. I just know that you'll either freeze to death or catch a fever.

Frank Soon as I've got enough money for some decent clothes, I'm going to find a proper job. I got the boots already. Look.

Liza I can buy you clothes. I can give you a home.

Frank turns his back on Liza

My circumstances 'ave changed. I've got a regular gentleman. A real toff. 'E gives me enough every week to rent my own place. It's not far away — Pinchin Street in Whitechapel. You'd like it. It's real cosy — and it's all mine, I don't 'ave to share. ... Oh, don't be like this, Frank. This is my chance. And yours, too.

She puts a hand on his shoulder but Frank shrugs her off. Liza turns to Annie

Well, what would you do, Annie? You know what it's like. There's hundreds of us — thousands, probably, with a bad start in life. Dad kicked me and Frank out on the street when Frank was only six. I took care of 'im as best I could, and I'm still trying. Maybe the wrong way — I don't know … it's funny. I see people all around so much worse off than me. Last night fer instance. I was in a pub near the Opera House with my gentleman, and this old woman came in, begging. Well, she was trying to sell flowers, but she only 'ad a few wilted bunches of violets. She shuffled in, wheezing like a pair of old bellows. Her face was all twisted, like she'd 'ad a stroke or something, and you should 'ave seen 'er hands. She could hardly hold the flowers. So I says to my gentleman, "Don't take the poor old woman's flowers, just give 'er the money." So 'e does, and she were that grateful she 'ad tears in 'er eyes, and then she kissed my hand — imagine it — and then she mumbled, "May God forgive you, my dear." (*Pause*) She were grateful — but at the same time, she pitied me.

Pause

Annie So what's this gentleman like then, Liza?
Liza He's all right. He is a proper gentleman. Some sort of lawyer with a big house near Chancery Lane. 'E says I'm too young to walk the streets and I'm only to go with him now. Well, I don't mind that as long as he's good to me.
Annie Is 'e married?
Liza I expect so. They usually are.

Annie offers Liza a drink

Thanks, dear. (*Lifting the bottle*) There's usually some comfort somewhere. (*Looking round*) Who else is 'ere? Sir Henry! You'll cheer us up, won't you? Come on, let's 'ave a whirl!

She runs over to him, pulls him to his feet as he pretends to protest. They dance a furious polka, the others laughing and calling out as they clap in time. Maggie does not join in. She is jealous. At the end of the dancing, Sir Henry sweeps a gallant bow and Liza curtsies, laughing and breathless. Then she puts a hand to his face

What 'ave you done to yer face, love?
Sir Henry An unfortunate misunderstanding, that's all. Or that would be all, if I didn't have an audition for *The Castle of Fear* at the Vic this very afternoon. I cannot appear on the stage looking like this. (*He sighs*) Thus do my dreams vanish into thin air.

Liza Make-up. That'll do the trick. I'll help you.

Sir Henry Excellent! Why didn't I think of that? Like you, Liza, I must take my chance. I'll go to the theatre after all. Now I must prepare my audition piece.

Sal Oh, show us what you're going to do, Sir Henry! I never seen no acting before.

Sir Henry Well, I don't know ——

Annie Oh, please!

Liza Go on. It can be a rehearsal.

Sir Henry Very well. I shall give them my Othello. (*Looking round*) One moment. Maggie?

Maggie has been sulking, but the moment Sir Henry calls her she jumps to her feet

The corpse of Desdemona — if you please!

All the others gather round in a semicircle as audience. Maggie stretches out on the floor. Sir Henry turns away to prepare himself. During the following, he uses his cane as a sword. There is a lot of excited chatter. As Sir Henry is about to turn, Maggie sits up

Maggie Ssssssh!

Maggie lies down again. All are quiet. Sir Henry launches into the speech with great passion and an amazingly deep and resonant voice

Sir Henry "Behold, I have a weapon;
  A better never did itself sustain
  Upon a soldier's thigh: I have seen the day,
  That with this little arm and this good sword,
  I have made my way through more impediments
  Than twenty times your stop; but O vain boast!
  Who can control his fate? 'Tis not so now.
  Be not afraid though you do see me weapon'd;
  Here is my journey's end, here is my butt,
  The very sea-mark of my utmost sail.
  Do you go back dismay'd? 'Tis a lost fear;
  Man but a rush against Othello's breast,
  And he retires. Where should Othello go?
  Now, how dost thou look now? O ill-starr'd wench,
  Pale as thy smock! When we shall meet at compt,
  This look of thine will hurl my soul from heav'n,

And fiends will snatch at it. Cold, cold my girl!
Even like thy chastity.
O cursed, cursed slave. Whip me, ye devils,
From the possession of this heavenly sight!
Blow me about in winds! Roast me in sulphur!
Wash me in steep-down gulfs of liquid fire!
O Desdemona! Desdemona! Dead!
Oh! Oh! Oh!"

Sir Henry flings himself on Maggie. Tumultuous applause. Sir Henry rises and bows, then helps Maggie to her feet. He holds her hand and they both bow. Whistles and applause through the next three speeches

Maggie I didn't move, did I? I didn't hardly breathe, even.
Sir Henry A truly splendid corpse!
Sal That were beautiful! I don't know what it all meant, but it were beautiful!

There is shouting and banging on their ceiling from above

Annie You'll knock 'em dead at the Victoria. And when you play The Long-Lost Heir in *The Castle of Fear*, we'll pack the gallery, you see if we don't.

All cheer

Peg enters

Peg Oi! 'Old your noise, all of yer. You've gone and woken them upstairs. If there's any more noise, you're out! And I'll be joining yer, Ma Grogan says, if yer don't put a sock in it, so for pity's sake, settle down now and go to sleep.

Peg exits, grumbling

There are mutters and moans as the rest settle down. Sir Henry, Liza and Maggie stay seated, sharing out some more drink

Frank Annie, don't go to sleep. I want to ask you something.
Annie What?
Frank I went across the river today, to Rotherhithe, just for a change. I did the mudflat by the quay. I found something too good to take to the rag shop. Should I take it to the pawnbrokers? What do you think?
Annie Let's see it then.
Frank It were wrapped up in this shawl when I found it. Funny, that.

Frank unwraps a muddy shawl to reveal a poker

Sal What's that Frank's found?
Annie It's a poker. Heavy. Sure to be worth a bob or two.
Sal Let me see.

She takes the poker and stares at it

And the shawl. Give it here.

She takes it and examines it minutely

(*Quietly*) Oh my God.

Gingerly she puts the poker and shawl down

That's what she done it with. That poker. And she was wearing that shawl.
All spattered with blood it was.

She sways. Annie and Maggie take hold of Sal and sit her down

Maggie Put yer 'ead between yer knees. That's it.
Frank Are you sure that's the poker she done 'im in with?
Sal Certain sure. I used the thing every day. And that's her shawl. I know it
   is.
Frank She must 'ave thrown it in the river at high tide. The quay is only a
   few streets away from Albion Terrace.
Annie It's evidence, isn't it? We should take it to the police.
Liza It's evidence all right, but it don't necessarily prove that Mrs Saunders
   did the murder. Someone could have stolen the shawl to wrap the poker in.
Sal She'll say it was me!
Frank There's something else ...

They all look at Frank expectantly

Liza Come on, Frank — spit it out.
Frank I wasn't going to show yer this. I were going to keep it. (*He holds out
   a dirty pocket-book*) There's money in it. Quite a lot.
Sal Money? He had money? And he didn't tell her? 'E might be alive right
   now, if she'd known he had some cash ... She can't 'ave looked inside the
   pocket-book.
Sir Henry No, I think she was so intent on making it look like a robbery, that
   she just took it and got rid of it, with the poker. She must have been in a
   panic, because there was no real need to throw away the poker. But then,
   she probably only thought of blaming you later.

Pause

Annie So, is the pocket-book and the money proof that Sally didn't do it? What would your lawyer gentleman say, Liza?

Liza I'm not sure. What I do know is, from listening to 'im talk, is that once you're in court, those barrister blokes can twist your words and make you look guilty even if you're pure as driven snow. I think Sal should lie low still. But we should keep these things safe until I get a chance to talk to my gentleman about it all.

Maggie Where? Not 'ere. We 'ave to clear out by seven, and then Ma Grogan and Peg turn the place over, in case anyone's left anything behind worth pinching.

Liza I'll keep them at my place. (*She gathers up the poker, shawl and pocket-book, then looks round at the other sleeping children*) Don't tell anyone else about this. Just in case.

Sir Henry Liza, I'll come and see you before I go to the audition.

Liza Pinchin Street, don't forget. Bring your greasepaint and I'll do yer up a treat. (*Aside*) I don't suppose you could persuade Frank to come too?

Sir Henry I'll do my best, but I doubt he will.

Liza I'll be off then. Sal, don't go anywhere on yer own. Safety in numbers, eh. Chin up.

Liza exits

The rest settle down. Maggie blows out the candle. There is some grey light, and the sound of birdsong

Sir Henry Dawn. "But look, the morn in russet mantle clad, Walks o'er the dew of yon high eastern hill".

Annie Looks like another grey day to me. (*She settles down, yawning*) And there ain't no 'ills in Wapping ...

Sal The birds don't sing like they do at home. You'd never know it were spring in London. There'll be blossom on the apple trees now, and the pasture coming up so green. And the hedges white with may. I wish you could see it, Annie. One day I'll take you there, I promise ... I were thinking about what Liza said, about so many children not having homes and families, and having to fend for theirselves. And I thought, well, I've got a home and family, so I'm lucky ... And then I thought, well, as soon as my younger sister was old enough to look after the little ones, 'stead of me, they packed me off to London, to work for Mrs Saunders, so there would be one less mouth to feed. And I wonder ... even if I did manage to get back to the village ... would they even be pleased to see me? ... What do you think, Annie?

Annie and the others are asleep

Annie?

The birdsong fades. During the scene change the song "Blow Away the Morning Dew"

Song: Blow Away The Morning Dew

Upon the sweetest summer time
In the middle of the morn,
A pretty damsel I espied,
The fairest ever born

Chorus
And sing blow away the morning dew,
The dew and the dew,
Blow away the morning dew,
How sweet the winds do blow.

The yellow cowslip by the brim,
The daffodil as well,
The timid primrose, pale and trim,
The pretty snowdrop bell.

Chorus
And sing blow away the morning dew,
The dew and the dew,
Blow away the morning dew,
How sweet the winds do blow.

She's gone with all those flowers sweet
Of white, of red, of blue,
And unto me, about my feet,
Is only left the rue.

SCENE 3

The river

There is the rippling sound of water

The Lights come up on Sal, Annie, Frank and Mouse mudlarking. Annie is coughing and shivering. Frank and Mouse grab different ends of the same piece of rope

Frank Oi! Mouse! That's mine!

Mouse doesn't answer, just hauls determinedly on the rope

I said, it's mine. Let go.

Frank is dragging Mouse towards him

You pig-headed halfwit! Will — you — let — go!
Sal Let her have it, Frank. You got plenty of stuff today, and she's got hardly nothing.
Frank So what. I saw it first.

Annie notices what is going on. She wades to Mouse and takes hold of her end of the rope. Mouse lets go, nursing sore hands. Annie tugs at the rope

Annie Come on, Frank, let us 'ave it. You don't need it as much as Mouse.
Frank Yes I do. I got nearly enough money for a suit of clothes. This rope's mine.
Annie No — it — ain't!

They struggle, grunting with effort. Annie starts to cough

Sal, come and help me.
Frank That ain't fair!

He lets go of the rope, suddenly. Annie falls backwards into the mud. Sal and Mouse hurry to help her. Frank grabs the rope and his basket

Serves you right!

Frank wades to the bank and exits

Sal and Mouse drag Annie towards the steps

Jericho enters

Jericho What's happened? 'Ang on. I'll help yer. (*He climbs down from the bank*)

Sal Clear off, Jericho. We don't want no help from any of King's gang. Not
after what you did to Sir Henry.

Jericho I were sorry fer that, after. And I come to warn yer ...

Sal Let go of Annie. And go away. We don't trust you, and we don't need
you.

Jericho All right, all right, Spitfire. I'm going. But I'm warning you, King's
got it in fer you and Annie, so watch out.

Jericho exits

*Annie and Mouse scrub at Annie with their shawls and skirts. Annie is
coughing and spitting and shivering uncontrollably*

Sal Look at you! You're covered in mud.

Annie Just get me to the pump.

Sal You're shivering, and it's not even cold.

Annie I just got Mouse's cough, that's all. I'll be all right.

Mouse Tide's coming in.

Annie So it is. We'd better call it a day. And it's the chimney sweeps' May
Day. Mustn't miss that. They'll be dancing down the High Street.

Sal We celebrate the first of May in our village! What's it like here?

Annie You'll see. (*Coughing*) Help me up again. Look 'ow fast the tide's
coming in. The flat we were working is already cut off ... I found a body
'ere once.

Sal How awful.

Annie Yeah ... it was. I saw this piece of rag sticking out of the mud, and
I pulled at it and this hand come up. Black and bony, like a claw. I could
see it 'ad a ring on one of the fingers, but I couldn't touch it. Frank would
'ave 'ad it, you can bet yer life.

Sal What did you do?

Annie I just let it slide back into the mud. Didn't tell no-one. No point.
Probably a suicide come down from Waterloo Bridge. (*Coughing again*)
That's the favourite place.

Sal Come on, let's get you clean. Then we can cheer ourselves up watching
the sweeps dance.

Annie You're a good friend, Sal.

Sal You've been so good to me. I wouldn't have lasted five minutes on the
streets without you.

They pick up their findings and start to move off

Did I tell you I'm going to take you home with me one day, so you can see
the real country? So you can see the animals in the fields, and the apples
growing on the trees and the clean-flowing river?

Mouse tugs at her sleeve

Yes, you can come too, Mouse. There's no mud under our river, just sand and stones, and it's so clear you can see the weed and the fish. We'll go fishing with my brothers, and we'll go apple scrumping, or if it's June we can help with the hay-making ...

They exit

There is a solo reprise of "Blow Away The Morning Dew"

Song: Blow Away The Morning Dew (Reprise)

Upon the sweetest summer time
In the middle of the morn,
A pretty damsel I espied,
The fairest ever born

Chorus
And sing blow away the morning dew,
The dew and the dew,
Blow away the morning dew,
How sweet the winds do blow.

The yellow cowslip by the brim,
The daffodil as well,
The timid primrose, pale and trim,
The pretty snowdrop bell.

Chorus
And sing blow away the morning dew,
The dew and the dew,
Blow away the morning dew,
How sweet the winds do blow.

She's gone with all those flowers sweet
Of white, of red, of blue,
And unto me, about my feet,
Is only left the rue.

Scene 4

Wapping High Street

From a distance there is the noise of the procession. The Sweeps are banging shovels, pots, tin trays, etc. with their wooden sticks. The noise gets closer

The Sweeps and the May King and Queen enter. All have black faces and flowers twined round their hats and pinned to their jackets. They are followed by Maggie, Goose, Jack, Jericho, King, Frank, Liza and Sir Henry. All sing the May Day song with gusto

Song: Rise Up Jack (The May Day Song)

Rise up, Jack, and sing your song
The summer is short and the winter's long!
We'll all join hands and form a chain,
Till the leaves of Springtime bloom again!

The Sweeps take their places for their dance

Sal, Annie and Mouse enter

They are on the opposite side of the dancing area to Sir Henry. The crowd is chattering happily as the Sweeps get to their positions and their musicians sort themselves

Annie We 'aven't missed it! I 'ate to miss this, Sal. It's like the start of summer, and nothing seems so bad in the summer. (*She coughs*)

Sal Oh, Annie, you're so cold and wet ... Here, put my shawl and bonnet on, or you'll catch your death. (*She gives them to Annie*)

Sir Henry (*waving to catch their attention*) Annie! Annie! I got the part! The Long-Lost Heir! I start rehearsals tomorrow!

Annie I knew you would! Well done, Sir Henry! (*She puts on Sal's bonnet and shawl*)

Music: Old Joe Clark (Sweeps' Dance)

The music and dance begin, a simple Morris dance, using the sticks. Everyone claps in time to the music and moves around to get better positions, so that Sal becomes separated from Annie

Mrs Saunders enters, a still, ominous figure among the revellers

King approaches her. They exchange a few words, King pointing at Annie. The Sweeps' Dance ends with a leap and a shout. The dancers crouch and pick up their pots, trays, etc. One begins to bang with a repeated rhythm, another joins in with a counter rhythm. Gradually the dancers all join in the percussive racket

> *At the height of the noise, Jack-in-the-Green bursts into the middle of them to shrieks and cheers from the crowd. He carries over himself a light-weight frame covered in leaves. The effect is one of a dancing bush*

The crowd press together closer to watch. Mrs Saunders, Annie, Maggie, Frank are on the upper level. Jack-in-the-Green dances round the Sweeps, they now all beat in the same insistent rhythm, at the climax of which Jack-in-the-Green collapses to the ground. Pause and silence as all are focused on the dancer, during which Mrs Saunders, with a hand over Annie's mouth, stabs her in the back. Nobody sees this, except King who has been watching Mrs Saunders all the time

> *Mrs Saunders exits*

Annie collapses, face down. Starting quietly the Sweeps beat a rapid rhythm to a loud crash as Jack-in-the-Green comes to life again by leaping up. All cheer. The dancers bow. One of them starts to collect money from the crowd. Jack-in-the-Green emerges from his frame to accept an offered drink

Maggie *(kneeling by Annie)* Sal? What's the matter, Sal?
Frank That ain't Sal, is it?
Sal *(joining them)* What's going on? Annie? I knew it! She's got a fever. *(She kneels by Annie and puts a hand on her back, meaning to turn her over)* Oh, my God! She's bleeding! Annie — Annie!

Sal and Maggie turn her over

Maggie Someone's stabbed her. Look!
Liza What's wrong with Annie?
Sal She's hurt real bad. We got to stop the bleeding. Help me.
Sir Henry Wait a moment.

He kneels by Annie and puts his hand over her heart. The crowd has noticed that something is amiss

Stand back, all of you. And be quiet.

He listens for any sign of breathing, then takes out his mirror and holds it above her mouth. He straightens up and shakes his head. Pause

Sal (*quietly*) No. She can't be.

The group is very still

Jack-in-the-Green What's going on?
May Queen Someone's croaked it. Let's move on.

The Sweeps, Goose and Jack and others slip away quietly

The group round Annie is very still. King remains a little detached from them. Sal crouches by Annie, holding her hand

Sal Annie? ... Annie?
Maggie (*gently*) She's dead, Sal. There ain't nothing you can do.

Mouse starts to cry and is comforted by Liza

Sal We can't just leave her here in the street.
Maggie We should get the peelers. This is murder, this is! And they'd take care of Annie.
King No!

They all turn to look at him

I got a better idea. This bloke I know, he'll take 'er.
Liza Why? Where to?
Sir Henry (*suspiciously*) Yes, where is this bloke of yours going to take her, King?
King (*after a pause*) Guy's Hospital. They'll give you two whole guineas for a fresh corpse.
Sal ⎰ (*together*) No!
Mouse ⎱
Liza You take the biscuit, King! Make money out of Annie being dead. My God, I'm an honest woman compared to you!
Frank You tell 'im, Liza!
King I was only trying to help.
Jericho (*strongly*) Oh no you wasn't!

All focus on Jericho

You gone too far this time. You're 'eaded for Newgate, King, and I ain't coming with yer.

King 'Old yer tongue, Jericho, or I'll make yer.
Jericho Oh yes? Look around you. Where is your protection? Whippet in the clink, Plug gone off, don't know where. And the others? I don't see 'em.
King This is all the thanks I get ——
Jericho Thanks? You don't get thanks fer what you've done. (*He looks round at the others*) Do you know what 'e done? Informed that Mrs Saunders where Sal's bin 'anging out — fer money! No wonder 'e don't want the police coming.
King I never! He's lying!
Jericho That's why Plug left. And I'm going too.

Jericho exits

Liza So it could 'ave been Mrs Saunders that stabbed Annie ...
Maggie Thinking it was Sal!
Sir Henry Because she was wearing Sal's bonnet and shawl ...

They stare in horror at King. Suddenly, Sal erupts into a scream and launches herself at King, beating him with her fists and sobbing hysterically. Maggie and Sir Henry pull her off. King stands panting and looking frightened

Liza Run, King. Go on. Run like the rat you are.

King runs off

The others calm Sal down

Frank What we gonna do?
Maggie Poor Annie. We can't just leave her.
Sir Henry This is what we'll do. We'll carry her to the church in Scandrett Street. It's not far. The vicar always leaves it unlocked. And he's a good sort. He'll see she gets buried properly.
Sal Annie once told me she'd never ever been inside a church.
Maggie Sir Henry's right. It's a respectful place to leave 'er.
Liza And then you're coming with me, Sal. We'll go and see my gentleman and ask 'im what to do. We'll show 'im the pocket-book, the shawl and the poker, and explain everything.
Sal Will he believe us?
Liza I think so. If we tell 'im everything straight.
Sal (*after a little pause*) Yes, we'll tell him straight. The peelers, too. I can't hide no more. I got to stand and face it. For Annie.

Maggie, Sir Henry, Sal and Mouse lift up Annie. Liza looks at Frank and holds out her hand. Frank takes it and they walk off together after the others

There is a very quiet reprise of of the second verse of the song "Dark River"

Song: Dark River (Reprise)

> Invisible children in rags and bare feet,
> Our father's the river, our mother's the street.
> Hard blows for a teacher and hunger for nurse,
> Our playmate is fear and our names are a curse.
>
> Dark river, dark river, that flows to the sea,
> One day take me with you and let me be free.

SCENE 5

The street in Wapping

The street, as Act I, Scene 1

Mouse, not lit, is lying by the pile of rubbish. King, Jericho, Liza, Frank, Maggie (who leans on a crutch) and Sir Henry are in the shadows at the edges of the acting area. They step into the light as they speak in turn. During the following, all on stage, except Sal, repeat the last line of the speeches in a ghostly whisper

Sal enters in a smart coat, parlour maid's cap and gloves

Sal Two years since I lived by the river. This is the first time I've been back. I thought I'd look up old friends, but it's not easy. And there's a few I'm glad not to see.
King Like me, King. I'm far away from London. Can't touch you. Convicted as an accessory to the murder of Annie, mudlark, of no fixed abode. Sentenced to hang, but commuted to transportation to Australia on account of my youth — and the fact that I gave evidence against Mrs Saunders ... who did not escape the noose. At least it's warm out here, though I dare say there are those in Wapping who wish I was in a warmer place. They still call me King. No-one touches me fer dipping. When I've served my time, I'll work my passage back to England. I've a debt to pay. To Jericho.
All *To Jericho.*
Jericho 'E blabbed everything to the peelers about Mrs Saunders, thinking 'e could get off scot free. But I peached on 'im, about Annie. 'E knew all the time Mrs Saunders was out to kill you, Sal. I did try to warn yer. But

it all come out in court. Liza was right. Lawyers are artful. So, I ain't been back to the river. I'm apprenticed to a sweet-maker in Camberwell. I don't pick pockets no more. It's all sugar and spice for me.

All *It's all sugar and spice for me.*

Liza Yes, lawyers are artful. But my gentleman kept 'is word. You would 'ave 'ad a hard time with the peelers, Sal, if 'e 'adn't backed you up. Then, afterwards, 'e got that job for you out at Islington.

Sal I started out as kitchen skivvy — but I'm a parlour maid now.

Liza And he moved me into a really nice apartment and gave me a proper allowance. Frank lives with me now, and goes to school. He's getting on really well with reading and writing and calculating. He thinks he'll be a clerk and work in the city. I'm happy Sal. I've got all I ever wanted.

All *I've got all I ever wanted.*

Frank I've got ambitions. No more empty belly, no more chilblains, no more stinking mud. The only thing I'll get on my hands are ink stains — and the smell of money.

All *The smell of money.*

Maggie I ain't done so well, Sal, since the accident. Jack and me were on the crossing, and there was a lot of traffic and it was raining. We were arguing in the middle of the road about whose call it was, when an omnibus careers round the corner. The horses 'ad bolted. I got such a kick from one of 'em, my leg was broke in three places. I can 'ardly walk now. But Jack fell right under the horses and the wheels went straight over 'im. 'E didn't stand a chance. So I'm in the workhouse now and I don't think I'll ever get out. I'm in a room the size of a birdcage with a dozen other infirm women. Goose used to visit sometimes, but now 'e's left off sweeping and joined a circus as an acrobat. 'E travels a lot. I don't see 'im no more. I don't see no-one.

All *I don't see no-one.*

Sir Henry Remember me, Sal?

Sal How could I forget you, Sir Henry.

Sir Henry *The Castle of Fear* was the turning point for me. That, and growing another three inches. I've been in the regular, legitimate theatre ever since. No penny gaffs or public house performances for me! I play the dashing young hero now. 'The Unknown Bandit', 'The Soldier of Fortune', 'The Gypsy Prince' — I've played them all. True, I've not yet given my Othello, my Hamlet, or even my Romeo. But that will come. Drop by and see me soon, Sal, and I'll get you a ticket for the dress circle.

Sal I will, Sir Henry.

Sir Henry Mister Henry Granville is my stage name. Still rather aristocratic, don't you think? You'll see it on all the billboards outside the theatre — Henry Granville! A name to remember.

All *A name to remember.*

King, Jericho, Liza, Frank, Maggie and Sir Henry exit

Sal And who remembers Annie's name now? No-one claimed her body. When they talked about her in court, no-one even knew if she had a surname. Just Annie, mudlark, of no fixed abode. I suppose the river was her home ... I'm going home, for a holiday. The first time in two years. I had a letter. They say they've missed me ... I wanted Annie to see my river, the young, clear river, before it's made dark and dirty by the city ... I won't come back here again. There's nobody here for me any more.

Sal moves off

The light gradually comes up on Mouse. There are sounds of carriages

Mouse Sal? Is that you Sal?

But Sal has gone. Mouse shrugs her shoulders, coughs and pulls the sacking around her shoulders, then sticks out her hand, looking at the audience. The carriage sound effects crossfade into modern day traffic noises

Spare some change for a cup o' tea, mister ... lady ... give us some coppers ... Can you spare some change ...?

Mouse keeps repeating her begging whine under the roar of traffic

A Boy skates by on roller-blades. A City Gentleman with umbrella and newspaper under his arm passes near Mouse and tosses her a coin. From the other direction comes a Smart Woman who shakes her head at Mouse and hurries off. Two School-kids walk by, ignoring her as they chat and giggle over a magazine

... Spare some change?

The sound effects fade as the Lights fade to——

—— BLACK-OUT

FURNITURE AND PROPERTY LIST

ACT I
SCENE 1

On stage: Pile of rubbish, junk and old sacks

Off stage: Broken basket (**Annie**)

Personal: **King**: handkerchief

SCENE 2

On stage: Nil

Off stage: Broom (**Maggie**)
             Broom (**Jack**)

Personal: **Passers-by**: coins (optional)
             Jack: (coins)

SCENE 3

On stage: Pieces of mud-caked metal, bone, rope, etc.

Off stage: Filthy container (**Annie**)
             Filthy container (**Mouse**)
             Filthy container (**Frank**)
             Broom (**Sal**)

Personal: **Sal**: coins

SCENE 4

On stage: Baskets of apples, bloaters, turnips, watercress
             Tray of bootlaces
             Tray of gingerbread
             Push cart. *On it*: container of soups, ladle and soup bowls

Off stage: Hunk of bread, broom (**Sal**)
             Hunk of bread (**Annie**)
             Hunk of bread (**Mouse**)
             Hunk of bread (**Frank**)
             Pair of old boots (**Frank**)

Personal: **Sal**: coins
Annie: coins
Children: coins
Soup Seller: handkerchief

SCENE 5

On stage: Mattresses
Blankets
Pillows
Stool
Playing cards and coins for **King**, **Jericho** and **Plug**
Lighted candle

Off stage: Broom (**Sal**)
Lighted candle (**Peg**)

Personal: **Annie**: penny
Sal: coins
Frank: coins, bottle
Sir Henry: cane (carried throughout), newspaper, handkerchief
Liza: coins

ACT II
SCENE 1

On stage: Street lamp

Personal: **King**: clay pipe
Mrs Saunders: coin
Sir Henry: handkerchief, small mirror

SCENE 2

On stage: Mattresses
Blankets
Pillows
Stool
Playing cards, dice, etc.
Bottle of gin and bottle of beer
Cups, mugs
2 brooms
Penny whistle for **Peg**
Poker wrapped in a muddy shawl for **Frank**
Lighted candle

Personal: **Frank**: dirty pocket-book

SCENE 3

On stage: Pieces of rope
              Baskets/containers for **Sal, Frank, Annie** and **Mouse**

SCENE 4

On stage: Nil

Off stage: Shovels, pot, tin trays, wooden sticks, etc. (**Sweeps**)

Personal: **Sir Henry**: small mirror
              Mrs Saunders: knife

SCENE 5

On stage: Nil

Off stage: Umbrellas, newspaper, coin (**City Gentleman**)
              Magazine (**2 School-kids**)
              Crutch (**Maggie**)

LIGHTING PLOT

Practical fittings required: street lamp
Various interior and exterior settings

ACT I, Scene 1

To open: Spot on pile of sacks and rubbish

Cue 1	**King** strolls on with his gang *Bring up full exterior lighting*	(Page 1)

ACT I, Scene 2

To open: Spot on **Maggie**

Cue 2	**Maggie**: " … on yer toes!" *Bring up full exterior lighting*	(Page 6)
Cue 3	A whistle blows *Fade to black-out*	(Page 10)

ACT I, Scene 3

To open: Rippling effect into full exterior lighting

No cues

ACT I, Scene 4

To open: General lighting on **Costers**

Cue 4	**Soup Seller**: "Come and try it!" *Fade to spot*	(Page 13)
Cue 5	**Soup Seller**: " … toil-worn hand to another." *Bring up general lighting*	(Page 14)
Cue 6	**Annie** and the others run off *Black-out*	(Page 17)

ACT I, SCENE 5

To open: Spot on **Sal**

Cue 7	**Sal**: " … banging on the door." *Bring up lighting on **Annie** and **Mouse***	(Page 17)
Cue 8	**Sal** joins **Annie** and **Mouse** *Fade spot*	(Page 17)
Cue 9	**Peg** leads the way into the cellar *Crossfade to cellar area*	(Page 18)
Cue 10	**Sal** stands horror-struck *Black-out*	(Page 25)

ACT II, SCENE 1

To open: Practical on with covering pool of light

No cues

ACT II, SCENE 2

To open: Dim lighting on lodging area

Cue 11	**Maggie** blows out the candle *Grey dawn light gradually coming up*	(Page 37)

ACT II, SCENE 3

To open: Rippling effect into full exterior lighting

No cues

ACT II, SCENE 4

To open: General bright exterior lighting

No cues

ACT II, SCENE 5

To open: Pool of light

Cue 11   **Sal** moves off   (Page 48)
            Gradually bring up spot on **Mouse**

Cue 12   **Mouse**: "Spare some change?"   (Page 48)
            Fade to black-out

EFFECTS PLOT

ACT I

Cue 1   To open   (Page 1)
Sounds of carriage wheels, horses, footsteps

Cue 2   **King** and his gang stroll on   (Page 1)
Fade sounds of carriage wheels, horses, footsteps

Cue 3   **Annie** and **Mouse** carry off the sacks, etc.   (Page 5)
Bring up traffic sounds of horses, carriages, cabs, etc.

Cue 4   As Scene 2 begins   (Page 6)
Reduce volume of traffic sounds

Cue 5   **Jack** gives **Sal** a push   (Page 9)
Return volume of traffic sounds to previous level

Cue 6   **Jack** stands with his broom   (Page 10)
Fade traffic sounds

Cue 7   To open Scene 3   (Page 10)
River sounds; continue throughout scene

Cue 8   **Sal** and the mudlarks exit   (Page 12)
River sounds crossfade to street market sounds of carts,
barking dogs, loud talk, a hurdy-gurdy, etc.

Cue 9   **Soup Seller**: "Come and try it!"   (Page 13)
Fade street market sounds

Cue 10   **Soup Seller**: " ... toil-worn hand to another." (Page 14)
Bring up market sounds as before

Cue 11   At the climax of the fight   (Page 16)
Police whistle, fade market sounds

Cue 12   **Annie**: "Quick! Run!"   (Page 17)
Distant shouts and police whistles; hurdy-gurdy music

Cue 13   Black-out   (Page 17)
Fade music and whistles; clock strikes
   twelve under sound of rain

Cue 14	To open SCENE 5	(Page 17)
	Sound of rain; continue	
Cue 15	**Peg** leads the way into the cellar	(Page 18)
	Slowly fade rain effect	

ACT II

Cue 16	To open SCENE 1	(Page 26)
	Fog effect	
Cue 17	**King**: " ... a good look out."	(Page 26)
	Clock strikes three	
Cue 18	**Sal**: " ... but it were beautiful!"	(Page 35)
	Shouting and banging from above	
Cue 19	**Liza** exits	(Page 37)
	Birdsong	
Cue 20	**Sal**: "Annie?"	(Page 38)
	Cut birdsong	
Cue 21	To open SCENE 3	(Page 37)
	Rippling water; continue until scene end	
Cue 22	**Sal** moves off	(Page 48)
	Traffic sounds of carriages, horses, etc.	
Cue 23	**Mouse** sticks out her hand, looking at the audience	(Page 48)
	Crossfade into modern day traffic sounds	
Cue 24	**Mouse**: " ... spare some change?"	(Page 48)
	Fade traffic sounds	

Lightning Source UK Ltd.
Milton Keynes UK
UKOW06f1347171215

264915UK00011B/196/P